For the love of Parsley

A guide to your Bunny's most common behaviours

By Samantha Wright

MONOCLE BUNNY

March 2011 edition

Copyright © 2011 by Samantha Wright

ISBN 978-1-4467-9111-0

Cover design © by Samantha Wright
Book design © by Samantha Wright
Illustrations © by Samantha Wright

www.fortheloveofparsley.co.uk

For all the Bunnies in the world.

"For the love of parsley, in addition to being adorably worded, is extremely informative. Ms Wright's prose is cute and fun yet extremely knowledgeable and is written in a way you will remember important points. It is a must have for all rabbit owners, beginner and experienced alike, for a different perspective on your bunny's ways. I love the fact there is a simple and an expanded version of the explanations, which are easy to refer to for when that burning bunny question crops up - I will certainly be keeping my copy handy at all times and as a veterinary nurse with a keen bunny crowd, will be recommending it to all my bunny mad clients".

- Laura Slinger, RVN, MBVNA Veterinary Nurse Easipetcare, Burton on Trent, Staffs

"I got my copy yesterday, I'm a couple of chapters in and it's great! Everyone should read it before getting a bunny! I've owned rabbits for a few years and have quite a bit of knowledge but am still enjoying reading it."

– J.Kirtly, Experienced rabbit owner

"We ceased running Bracknell Rabbit Rescue four and a half years ago when we moved -we still run a small Rabbit Sanctuary though known as 'Dean Forest Rabbit Haven'. This book is excellent and has taken the basics we used to pass on to new owners and expanded them greatly. Adequate space, proper diet (instead of yukky rabbit muesli), toys, vaccinations-we would have happily handed a copy to each new owner instead of the five page care sheets we had produced ourselves."

- Tim & Sue Carr, Dean Forest Rabbit Haven

"Dan quick! Quickly, shhh come see" and "Hello Bunny, whatcha doin'?" are the two most common things I say since getting Morgause.

The sheer array of behaviours she throws at us day to day can be overwhelming. Bunnies seldom do anything on a whim. Generally everything is for a reason, however due to a slight rabbit-to-human communication issue, figuring out what it is exactly Bunny is trying to say is very difficult. The quicker you learn the language of your lagomorph the better you can care for them and the stronger your relationship with the wee ball of fluff will be. This relationship can span up to and over 10 years so you'd best get cracking on!

From casual 'hello's to inevitable 'I'm not feeling well's and not excluding all the temper tantrums and expressions of love and happiness, when you finally get a grip on the language you quickly realise Bunny never shuts up. For something that is nearly mute rabbits are constantly communicating with you.

This little guide has been put together to give you a half decent insight into all (well, the most common) of Bunny's little rabbity ways.

There are a multitude of pretty good rabbit books out there but they seldom have the information you really need- quick simple answers as to why your rabbit is acting in a certain way, so you don't need to spend 40 minutes panicking whilst searching online pet forums.

The minute I noticed Morgs was eliminating chalky urine I swear I knocked 5 years off my life with heart palpitations. 35 minutes of furious 'Googling' and an awful lot of reading later, I had my answer. I decided then that a guide to what to expect when owning a lagomorph would have been a lifesaver, a lot easier, not so traumatic and a damn sight quicker.

The explanations are offered either simply or with added bumph so if you want a quick straight answer you've got it and if you want the background you can have that too.

No frills. No pictures. Just the key to your Bunny's happiness.

You can read all of it, some of it or just find the bits you need.

So here it is. From one normal rabbit-owning human to another-

A guide to your rabbit's most common behaviours.

Hope this book helps solve the Riddle of the Lagomorphs

Love Sam + Morgs

contents

CHAPTER 5 - YOUR RABBIT'S MOST COMMON BEHAVIOURS -

CHAPTER 6 - SIGNS OF ILLNESS OR INJURY -

CHAPTER 7 - THE STRESS FACTOR -

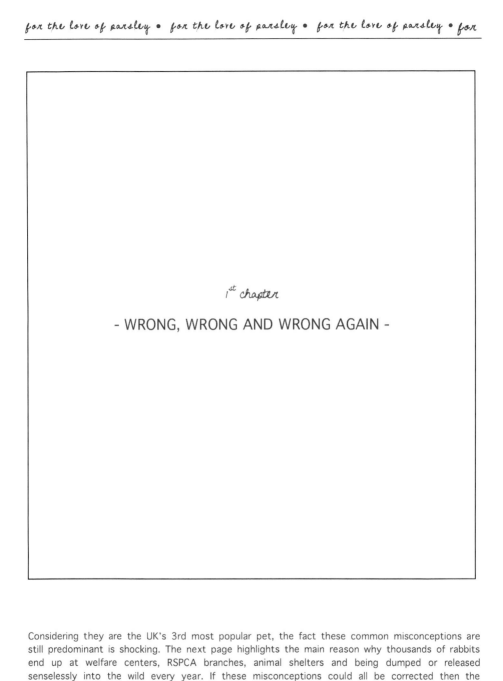

1ˢᵗ chapter

- WRONG, WRONG AND WRONG AGAIN -

Considering they are the UK's 3rd most popular pet, the fact these common misconceptions are still predominant is shocking. The next page highlights the main reason why thousands of rabbits end up at welfare centers, RSPCA branches, animal shelters and being dumped or released senselessly into the wild every year. If these misconceptions could all be corrected then the general welfare of rabbits would increase significantly worldwide.

CHEAP AND EASY
1st Common Misconception

Simply- They need lots of your cash, your time and your resources.

Bumph- Rabbits need constant attention, constant socialising, to be kept clean, dry, well fed with nutritional foods, have adequate toys, room, will need litter training if kept indoors and constant supervision if kept indoors. At the moment with VAT at 20.0% and the economy starting to settle a little after the economic crisis starting in 2008, my Netherland Dwarf Bunny costs me roughly £41 a month to keep (give or take £5) inclusive of:

▶ Nutritionally balanced food (both fresh and nugget)
▶ Pro-C supplements
▶ Hay (Timothy and forage)
▶ Bedding and litter

Then there are two vital vaccinations and spay surgery. Even at my well priced vets they total £65. Set up costs saw my bank handing out nearly £90 for:

▶ A suitably sized indoor cage
▶ Food and water crockery
▶ Seagrass mats
▶ A pet carrier
▶ 'Vetbed' material

As for time consumption, because she is an indoor rabbit she needs constant supervision when out and about in the house. Bunny-proofed or not, her inquisitive nature means she will get somewhere or something I don't want her getting her little mitts on. They also need to be observed carefully for any signs of illness, rabbits can degenerate over night if ill and medical intervention from a rabbit-savvy vet is always a must. Because she is currently also the only Bunny she depends on us for socialising. We are her herd, and she needs lots of time spent with her so she doesn't get lonely and despondent- plus what's the point in having a wee Bunny if I'm not going to spend time with her.

Rabbits also demand a lot of your patience, love and affection. Having such a huge personality in such a little being means they can sometimes really get on your wick, just like any other member of your family. Rabbits can be very testing, very moody and occasionally put me in mind of silent toddlers when they are tired and whiney and don't know what they want.

Rabbits kept outside need even more attention and it would be better for them if you have two so they could keep each other company, which means twice the cost and you will need to invest in a large run, shade or cover, possibly even more bedding to keep them warm, fly mesh for the summer and you will need to spend a lot of time outside with them to play and socialise.

GOOD PET FOR KIDS
2nd Common Misconception

Simply- Novelty soon wears off and more importantly rabbits and kids are by no means compatible.

Bumph- Prey animals are against loud noises, being chased, being caught, being roughed about and spend their entire lives avoiding it. Kids are loud, heavy handed, chase after pets, pick them up and then get hurt when Bunny thrashes out and bites them. Bunny will then log this event and start to get stressed and anxious in anticipation that it will happen again.

They may look cute and cuddly but 9 times out of 10 Bunny would rather be left on the ground and gently groomed or stroked. Children will seldom understand that the fluffy Bunny is not there for their pleasure, Bunny cannot be made to do what they wish and that Bunny will defend itself if necessary. Rough handling can result in broken bones, high stress levels and a very unhappy and aggressive rabbit. Loud noises will also produce a stressful environment; being chased and caught by a squealing child is probably one of the worse things a rabbit can think of. Being chased by a fox is less stressful. It is also unlikely that a young child will understand that Bunny needs their litter changing everyday, fresh water and food, playtime and rest time, grooming and careful observing for signs of illness and slightly older children are likely to soon get bored of the responsibility.

When the child is no longer bothered about the aggressive rabbit that doesn't want to know, it all falls down to the parent or guardian to take care of Bunny and unless you really want the animal the motivation to look after them properly can sometimes lack.

JUST KEEP IT IN A HUTCH OUTSIDE
3ʳᵈ Common Misconception

Simply- They need attention, grooming, talking to, playing with, 8ft by 8ft of running room minimum and a 6ft long shelter minimum.

Bumph- Keeping a rabbit outside seems odd to me given Bunny lives indoors with us. Although keeping Bunny outside would seem more natural, in doing so you are cutting off the social and emotional aspect, less you can get out there for 3-4 hours a day to play with Bunny and allow them the run of the garden. Keeping 2 bunnies together outside, as long as they have sufficient free running room, bedding, food, fresh water, shelter and toys would be ideal. However it is common to get a rabbit from a pet store because it looked cute, get it a small to medium sized hutch and put it in there in the garden and slowly forget it, especially when it's cold miserable and rainy and the last thing you want to do is go outside.

Rabbits have a need for speed, to jump, dig, bound about and play. They cannot do that in a hutch- even the minimum spec' ones. They need a good-sized run, they need toys, they need some form of companionship, social interaction and mental stimulation. A hutch alone is more like a prison than anything else as all it does is keep the rain off Bunny's head.

BORING PETS
4th Common Misconception

Simply- Rabbits are actually pretty nutty animals.

Bumph- This misconception arises from the fact that a lot of rabbits are kept cooped up sulking and bored witless in a hutch in the garden. If given the space, the time and the affection rabbits demand then you will quickly see that Bunny has just as much personality as cats, dogs, brothers and sisters.

They perform fantastic gymnastics, run around ridiculously fast, purr when happy, flop when ecstatic, throw toys about when playing, investigate anything they can get their little paws on and love being groomed or petted, some may even fight with you as to who gets groomed first. I have a hard time trying to groom my Bunny as she is always trying to groom me at the same time. They have the full range of emotions and express them very clearly; they even watch T.V with you. Rabbits are anything but boring, however if you do not give them the chance to be themselves you will never see it and the misconception for-fills itself.

SHORT LIFE SPAN
5th Common Misconception

Simply- Miserable rabbits live poor quality, short lives.

Bumph- 10 years and over. That is the life span of a happy, healthy, emotionally and mentally stimulated, nutritionally fed, well socialised and well treated Bunny. Naturally the span will vary from breed to breed but you are looking at anything from 8 years plus. In the wild due to illness, predators and in some cases pest-control, rabbits live 1-2 years.

If you get a Bunny, bung them in a hutch and forget about them, they too will live a shorter, unhappy life. Stress is a bunny's biggest killer and being looked after poorly just opens the door to a world of stresses. Adhere to the 5 freedoms, re-think these misconceptions, let Bunny express their natural behaviour, get a rabbit-savvy vet, the vaccinations and spay/ neuter surgery and share up to a decade of fun-filled Bunny-bliss with your lucky lagomorph.

2rd chapter

- LET ME INTRODUCE YOU TO YOUR RABBIT -

Arming yourself with the basics about your rabbit is the first step to understanding their behaviour. If you know the science and background behind the behaviour you have a better appreciation of the reasons 'why' and everything falls into place much quicker and with a lot more ease. I'm also just assuming Bunny is a house- bunny. Feel free to substitute 'house' for 'garden' and 'carpet' for 'grass'

... Though a rabbit chewing up the grass isn't a bad thing.

RABBITS ARE NOT RODENTS

Simply- Rabbits are categorised in an order (a rank in the biological classification hierarchy) called 'Lagomorpha' and Rodents in an order called 'Rodentia'.

Bumph- Rabbits are distinguished from rodents by a good couple of characteristics. The main being that although both classes have constantly growing teeth, rabbits have 4 incisors in their upper jaw. 2 sets, one smaller set nesting behind the other larger set. Rats, mice, squirrels, guinea pigs etc have one set of incisors. Rabbits are herbivores, their digestive system has adapted to only eating autotrophs (an organism that produces complex compounds, such as carbohydrates by using the suns energy) AKA plants. Hares and Pikas are known to dig into a piece of carrion when dietary supplementing is required. Rodents such as rats, Chinese hamsters and mice can eat meat as well as plants and have digestive systems built to deal with this omnivore diet. Rodents also have a penile bone with the scrotum sitting behind the penis- rabbits have no bone and the scrotum in front of the penis. Rabbits and rodents also walk differently. Like us rodents are 'plantigrade'- they walk with the sole of the foot planted flat on the ground. Rabbits are 'digitigrade' alike cats and dogs, walking on their toes. There are other physiological, skeletal, digestive differences but for now the above will do nicely.

YOUR PET RABBIT IS INHERENTLY THE SAME AS ITS WILD RELATIVE

Simply - This means that they express the same behaviour, have a digestive system adapted to deal with the same foods, have the same instincts and same welfare needs as wild rabbits, all of which need to be catered for by you.

Bumph- Your domestic bunny has remained the same as their wild relatives as far as instinct goes. They may have been bred for better temperament, different sizes and colours but when it boils down to raw nature there is no alteration. The environment they live in may have dramatically changed but the digestive system is the same, the foods they need to eat remains the same, they grow old and pass on the same, they still want to bound about, chew, dig and groom and they still need to socialise for enriched mental and emotional wellbeing. This in mind it's worth taking into account that the temper tantrums and evil streaks are still the same as well. What is different is species genetics, environmental interaction, knowledge of how to survive in the wild and their relationship with humans- because they are socialised and handled from birth, the domestic bunny will have a more trusting relationship with humans than their wild relatives who are naturally fearful. Life span is also a large difference. With proper husbandry (breeding practise) and care domestic rabbits can live up to 10 years and a little over, in the wild due to predation and illness many rabbits will live a year or two.

RABBITS ARE PREY ANIMALS

Simply- They are another hunting animal's food source.

Bumph- Your little ball of fluff is hard-wired for flight in a bid to save itself from being eaten. Because rabbits naturally have many predators they have evolved physically and mentally to keep themselves alive. As a result they are extremely alert, very reactive to their environment, skittish, built for bursts of speed and take a long while to gain the trust of. Prey animals have a large repertoire of anti-predation adaptations. A rabbit's main means of survival is 'avoidance'. Avoiding detection, attack and capture is the best means of avoiding being eaten. Rabbits' eyes are positioned on the side of their heads giving them a wider view of their environment and allowing them to be aware of what is going on at all times. Rabbits will freeze on seeing, hearing or smelling a threat, scan the area to assess the danger, thump their hind legs to sound the alert and burst into a zig-zagging sprint to evade chasing predators. If caught they have powerful hind legs to thrust and pound with and quite a nasty bite on them. Being a prey animal it also means that 9 times out of 10 rabbits hate being picked up. Being removed from the ground when your main defence is to run away is very stressful- essentially you are capturing your rabbit so do not be surprised when bunny reacts by kicking out violently and nipping you. They do not appreciate loud noises, sudden movements or rough handling because they are prey animals. For effective escape they need to leap straight into a sprint; this is facilitated by having a light skeletal structure and this means rabbits have very delicate bones and rough handling can easily break them.

RABBITS ARE USUALLY MOST ACTIVE AT DUSK AND AT DAWN

Simply- Generally, your rabbit will be most active first thing in the morning and mid-evening.

Bumph- For any Twilight fans out there you will be delighted to know that your rabbits are finely tuned to twilight. Twilight hours anyway. These are the hours between dawn and sunrise and sunset and dusk. This crespular (Latin derivative meaning 'Twilight') activity is more than likely to have evolved along side your prey animal's anti-predation adaptations. A rabbit's predators are most likely to be hunting a night or midday- rabbits have adapted to staying out of the way at these times and instead go mad when the risk of being hunted is reduced during twilight hours. Their body clocks respond to light conditions. As the light intensity varies throughout the day with the movement of the sun your rabbit's body clock can keep track of the time of day. In your home however it can be a little difficult to read the time of day with the artificial lighting so you may see your rabbit active in little spats throughout the day as opposed to during actual twilight hours.

RABBITS SPEND MOST OF THEIR DAY DIGGING, CHEWING, EATING AND SLEEPING

Simply- When they are not avoiding predators, sleeping soundly in their burrows (or cage), bunny will be busy digging at the carpet, chewing at any accessible wires and eating endlessly.

Bumph- These are all natural, instinctive behaviours. Your rabbit will always do it, needs to do it and nothing will stop them doing it. They will not understand you telling them off for it, it's like telling a lion off for roaring. It is what a rabbit is and you cannot reprimand it for being itself. The digging relates to digging burrows, digging up roots and foraging for food, the chewing relates to chewing the roots to remove them from tunnels and passageways they have just spent hours digging. Rabbit's teeth are endlessly growing and the chewing will help keep them in good condition. Rabbits also like to bunch materials up, scrunch materials up, shred materials and chew anything they can fit in their mouth, they are extremely curious and always investigating. Rabbits also spend a lot of their time eating. Sounds boring, but it is necessary. Given how energetic they are they haven't really chosen the best diet to fuel themselves, as a result they need to be constantly eating plants in order to get enough carbs' to power their little rabbity-ways. Power naps are essential as well, keeping an eye on their surroundings means being awake and alert for as long as they are in potential danger. Although bunny will still have one eye or ear on the environment they still catch 50 winks when possible. Between eating, shredding, bunching and chewing they will be dozing. They will also spend more than the owner's desired time marking territory with urine and pellets. As bunny gets older the intensity of these activities will decrease, but it's just easier to accept now that your home is in your Bunny's hands... well, jaws.

A RABBIT NEEDS TO LEARN ABOUT HUMANS AND LEARN ABOUT THEMSELVES

Simply- Rabbits are highly intelligent and need to learn about humans and how they differ from their own species.

Bumph- You will soon find out how disturbingly intelligent your rabbit is. Rabbits are not just panicky grass munchers. They are constantly taking in details, sights, sounds, smells and assimilating them. They pick up things very quickly, learn your morning routines before work; gaining an understanding about your interaction with them and learn that you provide the food, the water, the toys and the attention. They understand who is who in the family, which smell and tone belongs to who. They will gain an understanding of who is best for snuggles, who is best to play chase with and who is just best avoided. They will learn their names- or at least the sound and tone, they will learn where they are and are not allowed to go, what space is theirs and what space belongs to you. There is a lot for them to learn but they do it very quickly and all whilst scanning the environment for those pesky dangers. They have to learn just as much about you as you need to learn about them. What makes their intelligence even more disturbing is that they understand us on a basic level better than we understand them. They also need to learn about themselves. This happens before they are normally sold as kits. Breeders separate them from their mothers at around 8 weeks, but in this time they must learn all there is to learn about a rabbit that isn't innate so they have the social skills, experience and ease of bonding. If they aren't able to do this they are left a little confused and can be aggressive and undesirably temperamental later.

3ʳᵈ chapter

- THE FIVE FREEDOMS -

These are the five essential freedoms that you as an owner are legally obligated to provide for your rabbit, or any animal for that matter.

YOUR RABBIT'S WELFARE IS SO IMPORTANT THAT IF YOU NEGLECT THESE 5 BASIC FREEDOMS YOU COULD BE BANNED FROM KEEPING ANIMALS FOR LIFE, BE FINED £20,000 OR ISSUED A JAIL TERM OF 51 WEEKS.

Very simply and bluntly- If you cannot ensure all 5 are provided, for whatever reason, then really you should consider **not** owning the pet; that and you'll be breaking the law.

Legal bumph- O.K. Originally the basic 5 freedoms had been established in 1979 in the UK by the Farm Animal Welfare Council to assess the welfare of farmed animals. Since then they have been elaborated on, changed and improved vastly to include a more succinct list of higher welfare requirements that we see in our legislation now. Before that the only law protecting animals on any level was the Protection of Animals Act 1911 that simply said you cannot deliberately cause harm to the animal, this was inclusive of not seeking appropriate medical help. Even 100 years on the laws only stated you could not cause harm to an animal despite 20 odd other legislative pieces being in place.

In 2006 the UK Government finally pulled together and updated almost 2 decades of animal legislation and passed the Animal Welfare Act. This act meant those responsible for absolutely any living vertebrate animal had a duty of care to provide a suitable environment, a suitable diet, the ability to exhibit normal behaviour patterns, and protection from pain, suffering, injury and disease.

It might be worth adding here that by 'those responsible' it includes parents or guardians of those under 16, so even if Bunny is for your 13 year old, you are legally responsible for it.

FREEDOM FROM HUNGER AND THIRST
1ˢᵗ Freedom

see also...
Foraging p.26
Eliminating p.25
Droppings p.24
Cost p.2

Simply- Providing nutritionally balanced and appropriate foods at all times and clean, fresh water at all times.

Bumph- Sounds simple enough but it is paramount for Bunny's digestive health and overall wellbeing that you provide the right foods at the right age. After 7 months Bunny will need a high-fibre-low-protein diet. This means an unlimited supply of hay and grasses daily, the right fresh vegetables daily and the right dry nuggets daily is an absolute must. Do not buy the pretty muesli mix bags. They are not nutritionally balanced and encourage selective eating by Bunny. This means Bunny will only eat the bits they like the most and leave the rest; and having a sweet tooth Bunny will more than likely favour the sugary elements over anything else. This is not a well balanced diet and will leave Bunny deficient in vital fibre, minerals and vitamins. In turn this will upset their digestive tract, upset the delicate flora and bacteria in the cecum and lead to an unhealthy, unhappy rabbit.

FREEDOM FROM PAIN, INJURY AND DISEASE
2nd Freedom

see also...
Noises p.32
Eliminating p.25
Aggressive behaviour p.18
Cost p.2

Simply- Not to deliberately harm Bunny and to seek appropriate medical help when necessary.

Bumph- Bunny will let you know when they are in pain or discomfort if you pay attention.

Droppings are little windows into your Bunny's health. Keep an eye on how much Bunny is eating and drinking and the form, consistency and frequency of their droppings. It sounds like an odd conscious effort to be making but after a week of doing it you will find it's no more a conscious effort then it is a normal observation you make whilst saying "Good Morning" to Bunny and changing their water.

Also pay attention to Bunny's behaviour. Not wanting to be touched and expressing discomfort both physically and audibly when stroked or moving is a clear indication that something is not right. Sadly there is a vast array of illnesses and injuries that a rabbit can suffer and when ill rabbits degenerate very quickly. Register them with a rabbit-savvy vet, get them vaccinated against Myxomatosis and Viral Hemorrhagic Disease (regardless if they are outside or house rabbits), at 6 months book them in for spay/ neuter surgery and under no circumstances must you ever discipline your rabbit physically.

FREEDOM FROM DISCOMFORT
3^{Rd} Freedom

see also...
Cost p.2
Bunny 500 p.20
Binkies p.19

Simply- Provide an appropriately sized home and space to play.

Bumph- They can run fast, jump high and love to play. They cannot do that in a small compact hutch, they cannot do that in a space smaller than 8ft x 8ft. You need to provide them with a shelter, be it indoors or outdoors, where Bunny can retreat to and be housed in securely. This accommodation must protect them from the extreme cold and from drafts. It must offer relief from heat and keep Bunny bone-dry and it must also protect them from other pets and children.

FREEDOM FROM FEAR AND DISTRESS
4th Freedom

see also...
Aggressive behaviour p.18
The Stress Factor List p.47

Simply- To provide an environment where Bunny will not be pestered and harassed or stressed by any means.

Bumph- Just as when ill or injured, Bunny will let you know if they are scared, stressed or unhappy. You will be able to back-track events leading up to the behaviour that Bunny is using to communicate their unease with. You can then addresses the issues as necessary.

Rabbits also have incredibly memories. They will anticipate stressful instances reoccurring and act accordingly to defend themselves. If Bunny had a stressful experience being picked up, they will bite, growl or flatten themselves with their ears back to communicate that they do not like it when someone attempts to pick them up again. Do not continue to force Bunny to do things they express a dislike for. If this means moving Bunny away from other pets, housing them somewhere else or stopping young children from interacting with them etc then do so.

FREEDOM TO EXPRESS NORMAL BEHAVIOUR
5th Freedom

Simply- To allow Bunny to be Bunny, no-holds-barred.

Bumph- Any lack of provision that would otherwise allow Bunny to be Bunny is a restriction on their normal behaviour. Not providing a means for them to dig or chew recreationally, to socialize or play, to stretch out or groom will leave you with a very frustrated Bunny who's behaviour will turn aggressive as they cannot act as their nature dictates. Rabbits like any other animal have species-specific behavioural traits- that's what makes them a rabbit. Rabbits have evolved to dig and chew, to thump when there is danger, to bite and lunge when threatened. It is what Rabbits are meant to do. If you do not want an animal that acts in this manner then don't get a Bunny. Your skirting boards will inevitably get nibbled and the carpet's corners dug up- Bunny isn't being deviant and nasty with intent, they are just being themselves in the environment they were put in. You can try and compensate and provide alternative things to dig etc but at the end of the day if you find this behaviour unmanageable then a Bunny probably isn't best for you.

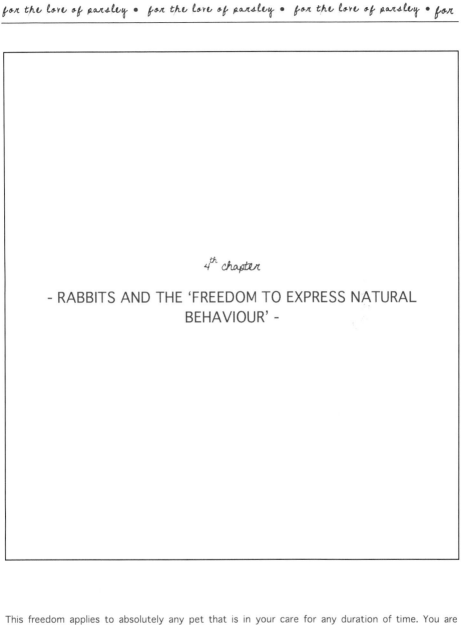

4ᵗʰ chapter

- RABBITS AND THE 'FREEDOM TO EXPRESS NATURAL BEHAVIOUR' -

This freedom applies to absolutely any pet that is in your care for any duration of time. You are taking an animal out of its natural environment, domestic or not. However you cannot take the 'natural' out of the animal. They will have basic and instinctual behaviours that they need to express in order to be happy, in order to be them. If you take away any means of expressing these then the animal will become very frustrated and depressed and have a poor quality of life. We become unhappy and unwell it if we are prevented from socialising, eating nutritional foods or exercising and pets are no exception to this.

RABBITS AND COMMUNICATION
see also...
Noises p.32
Aggressive Behaviour p.18
Chin rubbing p.22
Urinating on the sofa/ bed p.38

Simply- For an animal that is generally silent they never shut up. They communicate through physical manoeuvres, ear movements, grunts honks and smells.

Bumph- It's no good shouting all about the place when you are a prey animal as you are only going to attract attention to yourself. Physically rabbits are not built to produce loud calls or noises. As a result Bunny communication is extremely quiet, almost silent, but by no means subtle. Rabbits have scent glands under their chin used for marking territory, strong urine used for marking and pellets for marking. When happy they express it through play, leaping and bounding and making very slight, very quiet honking noises or light grinding of their teeth (they even panic you half to death by flopping randomly on their sides when content). These mini goose noises accompanied with circular running motions express sexual excitement and courtship. They use their ears like semaphore flags, when alert and when annoyed. If in pain they can squeal, grunt or produce a loud tooth grind, be ready to lunge and bite or squash themselves flat against the floor in avoidance and disapproval. If you ignore what Bunny is telling you then your relationship will suffer and Bunny will get frustrated.

RABBITS AND SPACE
see also...
Bunny 500 p.20
Binkies p.19

Simply- They need a lot of it. Both private to sleep or snooze safely and to run around in like a mad-hatter.

Bumph- Rabbits are speedy things. They are built for sudden bursts of speed, jumping, hopping, digging and playing. They have powerful light-weight bodies that need to be exercised daily, preferably for as long as they want, but for 3-5 hours minimum. Exercise is essential for their health, wellbeing, fitness, digestive system and expending all that insane energy they have. A bored rabbit is not a good thing at all. They need the space to investigate, communicate, socialise and play. Hutches and cages should only be for shelter and not the be-all-end-all of the rabbit's living space. They need a bear minimum 8ft by 8ft of room just to exercise in. When you think a rabbit can hop and jump up to 6, sometimes 7 or even 8 feet you start to appreciate the room they need. They need space to just sit and have quiet, reflective, safe, alone-time in and space to bound about and flop. They must be able to periscope (stand upright on their hind legs), have room to lay full length and space that allows them to escape if they feel threatened. They also appreciate more than one cubbyhole, box or tray to snooze, rest and sit in. Hutches and cages should also be a minimum of 6ft long. If this is where they are going to be securely housed when they cannot be let out or supervised then they will need the hutch or cage to be big enough to lay, flop, stretch and periscope as well as house a few toys, their food and water without being cramped.

RABBITS AND SOCIAL EMOTIONAL WELLBEING

see also...
Grooming p.28
Licks p.29

Simply- Rabbits are social animals. They live in groups and bond through grooming, licks, playing and eating.

Bumph- Rabbits are inherently gregarious (appreciate living in groups) animals. They naturally arrange their herds into a matriarchy (hierarchy with the female at the top) system with a pecking order that follows. Females are not necessarily always the dominant Bunny in the house though. If you have 2 rabbits, one male one female, either one of them could be dominant. If Bunny likes and trusts you, you too will be ranked somewhere in the herds' pecking order. You'll be able to tell where you come in this order by the way Bunny socialises with you. A Bunny asking to be groomed or asking for attention or acknowledgement by lowering their head in front of your hand is the dominant Bunny and you should be honoured really that Bunny requests your grooming services. Grooming, petting, feeding treats, playing with and responding to Bunny's communications are all part and parcel of the bonding process and is essential for Bunny's social and emotional well being. By playing with and feeding yummy treats to Bunny you will very quickly learn about their insane little personalities. You will also learn how to talk back to Bunny, how and when you have offended them, annoyed them, pleased them and interrupted them doing something ridiculously interesting; you will form a strong a long lasting and rather profound relationship with Bunny that will last their entire life time. Whether they are stressy and independent, loving and snuggly, aloof and quirky your interaction with Bunny is paramount to their happiness and emotional wellbeing.

RABBITS AND INTELLIGENCE AND MENTAL WELLBEING

Simply- Rabbits are extremely intelligent and investigative and need toys, games and human interaction to keep them stimulated. You really do not want a bored rabbit on your hands, unless you wanted the carpet replacing.

Bumph- Bunny, being a prey animal is constantly aware of their environment and are very reactive to it. They have to be quick to learn, to adapt and to understand what is going on in their environment if they want to stay ahead of the hunter's game. Because of this rabbits are extremely intelligent. I'm not suggesting they're sitting under the table knocking out complex equations, but they are sitting there taking in everything they see, hear, smell and can get a hold of and working along side it, adapting to it if need be. They are ridiculously inquisitive, cautious and playful. They inspect everything, test everything and ensure everything is safe. They can be trained quite quickly to use litter trays, respond to their names, jump over hurdles, not to go into certain rooms or spaces, to respond to a certain word that in turn tells them to go back to their hutches or shelters, to understand when certain foods are available and to play certain games such as 'fetch', a lot of bunnies also like to flop out and what T.V. Learning through repetition and reward is very stimulating for rabbits as it gets their little grey matter firing; It also involves play, treats and socialising with you. It is also a massive house-saver. Bored rabbits are house-wreckers and can be aggressive due to frustration. Lots of interesting toys, lots of mental stimulation, lots of human interaction equals a very bright and bubbly Bunny.

A page for scribbles.

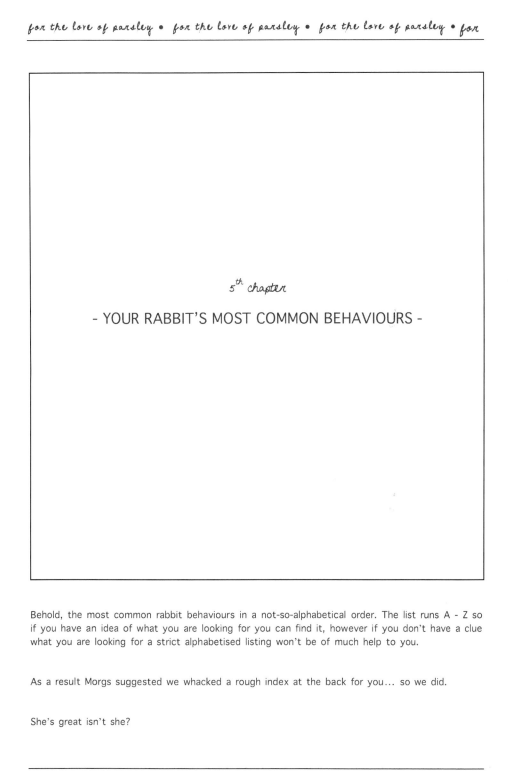

5th chapter

- YOUR RABBIT'S MOST COMMON BEHAVIOURS -

Behold, the most common rabbit behaviours in a not-so-alphabetical order. The list runs A - Z so if you have an idea of what you are looking for you can find it, however if you don't have a clue what you are looking for a strict alphabetised listing won't be of much help to you.

As a result Morgs suggested we whacked a rough index at the back for you... so we did.

She's great isn't she?

A is for...

AGGRESSIVE BEHAVIOUR

Bunny is a complete nightmare!

Simply - They're communicating with you that they are stressed, anxious or worried that something bad is going to happen to them or is currently happening to them. They may also be in pain from injury or illness. Check their droppings and urine for normality and make sure they are eating and drinking as normal too.

Bumph - Try not to think of it as aggression. Think of it as defence against something Bunny is scared of. You or someone has upset, angered, hurt or stressed Bunny out. This does not mean you have an evil renegade rabbit on your hands who hates you, it just means you need to stop whatever it is you are doing. Aggressive behaviour isn't an inherent trait for a social animal who loves spending hours on end chilling, snuggled up to herd members grooming. When a rabbit anticipates something negative happening to them or something triggers their anti-predator avoidance instincts they react by defending themselves. If this 'something negative' isn't addressed then Bunny will respond to the stress with consistently aggressive behaviour and become very unhappy and you will start to think Bunny is a nasty piece of work that you'd rather be without.

Under no circumstances should you punish or tell Bunny off. Bunny won't understand that you didn't intentionally scare or worry them, they won't understand the concept of an 'accident'. All they know is that it did scared them and they do not want a reoccurrence. Punishing them for being scared and defending themselves basically boils down to abuse as you are unnecessarily and unfairly stressing a prey animal further for instinctively protecting itself. Never hit your rabbit; never shout at your rabbit. A firm and authoritative "No" is more than satisfactory.

At the end of the day Bunny hasn't done anything wrong. The way you interacted with them just needs to be altered to remove the fear factor. Assess what is going on, listen to what Bunny is trying to tell you and carefully observe when the behaviour takes place. When Bunny expresses their unhappiness with a certain behaviour back-track what has happened leading up to the behaviour to figure out what is triggering it. When you have ascertained what is upsetting Bunny you can stop doing it, approach it a different way if necessary and reassure Bunny that it is O.K and that they are safe.

To give you a hand figuring out what made Bunny react you may want to look over the 'Stress Factor List' to see if you have overlooked something obvious. I do it all the time and often end up kicking myself.

ACTIVITY
Bunny is more or less active than normal

see also...
Ears as heaters p.25
The Stress Factor List p.47
Resting p.35
Signs of illness or injury #3, 4, 15 (pg.42)

Simply- Bunny could just be having a lazy week, be feeling a little under the weather or be in pain from injury and illness. Bunny may be a little too cool or hot and is cooling off/ retaining heat or it could be due to their body clocks reacting to changes in day-light as the seasons change.

Bumph- Rabbits are crepuscular. This means they are most active during twilight hours - at dawn and at dusk. In the UK at the moment that is roughly 07:20 and 17:00 (for January). Rabbit's body clocks are set to read light intensity, this lets them know what time of day it is and when their predators are less likely to be mooching about. However indoor bunnies have more artificial light than natural so their body clocks may be thrown off a little. Our lights are on and off all the time, Bunny will be use to this the on-off lighting as an event but as a means of telling the time of day she has to go by us letting her out, us feeding her and us putting her back to bed. Bunny also learns our work schedule - when we get up in the morning and when we get home. Rabbits are very habitual and like to stick to routines, if anything in that routine changes Bunny may express their confusion and annoyance.

Bunny could also just be having a lazy day. They are very much like us in that sense. Bunny may just want to chill out a bit more than usual, prefers dozing in a new safe spot or is just being very contemplative. On the other hand it could be an indication that Bunny is not feeling too well and should be observed a little more closely than normal in the event an illness is developing. Check their droppings and urine for normality and make sure they are eating and drinking as normal too.

Being more active could relate to them hitting sexual maturity, it being breeding season or Bunny hasn't quite had enough exercise as they need lately. Make sure Bunny is booked in for spay/ neuter surgery to prolong their healthy happy lives and make sure Bunny has 3-5 hours minimum a day to burn off all that energy and boredom.

Temperature may also have something to do with it. If the room is too hot or too cold then Bunny will be too. Check the room temperature and check Bunny's ears for a quick and rough indication of their body temperature. Hot ears equals a warm Bunny trying to dissipate some of the heat and cool ears equals a Bunny who is conserving heat.

B is for...

BINKIES
Jumping or hopping in the air sometimes mid run or mid activity
See also...
Signs of illness or injury #8 (pg.42)

Simply- Bunny is a very happy Bunny indeed.

Bumph- This is Bunny's way of communicating that they are happy, life is good and they are pleased with your hard-work. A binky is an unexpected jump in the air that often includes twists, head shakes, feet flicking and awkward landings. Many times we've watched our Bunny binky into the bookcase or even our legs as we sit innocently watching T.V. It looks like Bunny has suddenly been nipped by something but really it is just them expressing their joy and playfulness.

BUNNY 500

Running around as fast as they can manage, zig-zagging, hurdling and taking tight corners

see also...
Chasing p.23

Simply- Bunny is happy and practising some evasive manoeuvres in the safety of their environment. Get out the way quickly or stand damn still.

Bumph- Racing around the room as fast as they can manage whilst tearing up the flooring with their tight corners turns and hurdling is Bunny's way of saying they are happy, confident and much faster than you. You might even get an invite to play with them. In the wild rabbits will chase each other racing around the warren. It is good exercise and good for bonding and socialising, though I doubt you'll get much speed up yourself, more like a good couple of strides as Bunny runs off ahead almost giggling to itself, ears up and eyes wide and bright. Racing about with ears down is a negative display showing that Bunny is not enjoying themselves.

BITING

An expression of anger or fear that something negative is happening or is going to happen to them

see also...
Aggressive behaviour p.18
Nipping p.33
The Stress Factor List p.47
Signs of illness or injury #1 (pg.42)

Simply- Bunny is not happy about something. They either remember a past event that was unpleasant and anticipate it happening again or are defending themselves against an event that is currently taking place, they may also be in pain from injury or illness. Check their droppings and urine for normality and make sure they are eating and drinking as normal too.

Bumph- A bite from a rabbit hurts. A lot. You have had 2 sets of incisors with a very small surface area forced into your skin. This is Bunny's way of saying "Absolutely, 100% NO. Back off and stay away." Biting can occur with lunging, ears flattened back against their body and Bunny positioning themselves ready for bite or flight. You might be invading their personal space, irritating them, innocently attempting to stop them eating the skirting boards or positioning your hands in a threatening manner to them. Rabbits are prey animals with a wide field of view. If you rapidly rush your hands in front of their head, even if it is just to pet them, you will panic Bunny and they will react according to their prey animal nature.

Back-track the events leading up to the biting and try to think what occurred to make Bunny react in this manner. Don't think Bunny hates you; they are just acting as nature intended. If they didn't bite you wouldn't know you are doing something they really dislike. Remove the negative action and have gorgeous bite free hands.

BODY FLATTENED
A flattened tense body and flat ears when approached.

see also...
Aggressive behaviour p.18
The Stress Factor List p.47
Signs of illness or injury #1 (p.42)

Simply- Bunny isn't in the mood for grooming, petting or being picked up and would rather you just left them be. Stop your advances, retract your hand and leave Bunny alone to chill for a bit.

Bumph- The flattened tense body and flat ears is a sign of fear, if they could melt into the flooring for camouflage and protection they would. If they are expressing this when you are advancing to pick them up, simply stop and move away. Sometimes Bunny doesn't appreciate the snuggles and grooming. Rabbits can be quite temperamental like the best of us. If you aren't sure what has caused this instinctive reaction then back-track the events leading up to the behaviour and try to approach it from a different angle if necessary. Bunny could be having an 'off' day or they could be in pain from injury and illness or fearful of what is occurring. Check their droppings and urine for normality and make sure they are eating and drinking as normal too.

C is for...

CHEWING
Bunny is endlessly chewing things you do not want them to chew.
see also...
Digging p.24

Simply- Bunny proof your home as Bunny needs to chew to keep those teeth down.

Bumph- Wires, cables, carpets, skirting boards, books, shoes... we'd be here forever listing the contents of your home that will end up with teeth marks in it. In the wild, rabbits spend a lot of time chewing their food, the high-fibre diet helping to keep their constantly growing teeth nice and trim. In your home Bunny will be able to do the same with the constant supply of good quality hay you provide them with but they also need to chew recreationally. If your Bunny particularly enjoys chewing then you'll need to stock up on alternatives to chew. A wire or cable to a Bunny is a pesky tree or plant root that has infiltrated the warren. This needs to be removed to keep all escape routes clear. It is also the perfect size and shape to fit into Bunny's mouth, so ideal for chewing.

Move absolutely anything you do not want eating up and safely out of the way. Provide your little fluff ball with plenty of alternatives to chew. Apple twigs, willow sticks, willow balls, untreated wicker baskets, a book that really didn't do it for you, cardboard boxes/ tubes and tunnels, sea grass mats and natural loofahs to name a few. Some positive reinforcement and treat giving will also be required to help Bunny make the connection between good chewing things and bad chewing things.

However at the end of the day Rabbits will chew whatever they can fit in their little mouths' and will chew even more destructively if bored. Although you can reduce the undesirable behaviour you won't be able to eradicate what nature built in. Supervising Bunny's play time and lots of toys will help, as will a good sense of humour and a locked room to hoard your valuables in.

CHIN RUBBING
Bunny keeps sweeping objects with their chin.

see also...
Spraying urine p.36

Simply- That belongs to Bunny now.

Bumph- Under Bunny's chin there are scent glands and these are used to mark key objects and landmarks in Bunny's environment. It is a scent detectible only to other rabbits and lets them know that this area belongs to them and that that particular box, shoe, bookcase and chair leg also belongs to them. Chin rubbing is good for Bunny's emotional wellbeing and part of their territorial nature. You may find that when friends and family or strangers visit Bunny will chin rub insanely, this is to make sure everyone gets the hint and understands what belongs to Bunny, it also tops up the previous scent that may now be fading.

CECOTROPES
Bunny sits and eats its own poo!

see also...
Droppings p.24
Eliminating p.25
Leaving droppings inside cage p.30
Leaving droppings outside of cage p.31
Signs of illness or injury #2, 5, 6, 7, 10, 11, 12 (p.42)

Simply- Bunny's remarkable digestive system has done its job and produced a sort of rabbity-vitamin-suppliment, separate from the normal droppings, for Bunny to eat for a more efficient digestion. Ps they smell very, very strong.

Bumph- Tasty. Tasty and an essential part of Bunny's diet. You provide the nutritionally balanced nuggets, the unlimited supply of beneficial fibre in the form of hay and an unlimited supply of fresh clean water and Bunny will supply the mucuous-covered-mulberry of nutrients. Bunny doesn't digest food very efficiently first time round. In the wild these prey animals won't have time to get in all the food and nutrients they need so they eat little and often to maintain a healthy gut and keeping it in constant motion, then get all the nutrients later on in the day when it is safer. Not all Bunny's will pass these at the same time, it takes 4-8 hours to digest their food and the cecotrope will be passed anytime of day depending when Bunny has last eaten.

To facilitate this their digestive system has evolved to slightly back-track some of the half-digestive food through the large intestine, into a cecum sack and pack it full of bacteria so that when it is eventually passed, Bunny can quickly re-ingest it and break it down into more beneficial complex sugars, the rest of the food is passed as the normal droppings that you will be accustomed to.

Generally you'll seldom notice the 'night-time' droppings as Bunny is meant to gobble them up as they are passed. Even tastier. But occasionally Bunny will pass on eating them and leave them for your viewing pleasure. These self-made rabbity-vitamin-suppliments are essential to your Bunny's diet, they contain all the nutrients, bacteria and gut flora that Bunny needs to survive. This is why eating a high quality fibre is paramount to your Bunny's overall wellbeing.

CIRCLING FEET

Bunny runs around your feet, often grunting.

see also...
Nipping p.33
Grunting p.28
Signs of illness or injury #14 (p.42)

Simply- If Bunny is male and does it whilst grunting then he is in the mood for lurve. If female or no grunting is involved then Bunny is saying "Hi, I like you lots, come play with me".

Bumph- When male Bunny hits sexual maturity at between 3-8 months (depending on breed) he will start to express mating behaviour. Running around your feet only happens because when you stand up there is room to do it. Bunny is hard pushed to run circles around you when you are curled up on the sofa. In the wild male rabbits will court potential mates by running around them nipping and grunting. You should be flattered really that Bunny thinks you are genetically sound enough to mate with.

This behaviour will be curbed once Bunny is neutered. This is a good thing, not because you have stopped Bunny grunting and nipping at your ankles but because the neutering will extend Bunny's life expectancy and make life a lot more fulfilling for him. When reproduction isn't on the cards the circling of feet is an affection filled greeting, again be honoured because bunnies demand respect and acknowledgement and they must really respect and love you to express it.

CHASING

Bunny hops forwards a little then stares at you then hops forwards again

see also...
Bunny 500 p.20

Simply- Bunny is inviting you to play with them. Chasing Bunny whilst ears are up is joyous fun. Chasing Bunny whilst ears are down is not.

Bumph- In the wild rabbits love to play, to chase each other, to exercise those evasive techniques and get a bit of speed up. In your home it is no different... bar you won't be running anywhere. Watching my fellow human play chase with the Bunny is more like watching Bunny bounding about and a human awkwardly shuffling after them hindered by furniture. Bunny will invite you to play by beckoning you to go after them. Bunny will do this by sitting sideways on to you, hopping forwards a bit and waiting to see if you get the hint. If you didn't Bunny will repeat this.

The game of chase is only fun as long as Bunny's ears are up denoting happiness and enjoyment. The second they go down something is wrong, you've either scared them, advanced upon them too quick, startled them, annoyed them or initiated their anti-predator instincts. Just stop the chase there and wait on Bunny to tell you when they feel safe and relaxed enough to interact again. Not all rabbits will want to play, some might not appreciate the thrill of the mock chase, some just might not be interested in playing chase specifically with you and some would rather just destroy today's newspaper. It doesn't mean anything is wrong, it just falls down to Bunny's recreational preferences, age, health and wellbeing.

D is for...

DIGGING
Bunny digs at the carpet
See also...
Chewing p.21

Simply- Rabbits are inherent diggers and spend a lot of time doing it in the wild. Digging is fun and the only way tunnels get made. Bunny proof your home as Bunny will dig if you like it or not.

Bumph- These natural diggers love to dig, it is a life long mission and simple fun. You can provide alternatives to your carpet, upholstery and other cherished fabrics for Bunny to dig at. Giving some bunnies a fleece or towel of their own will see them scrunching, bunching and smoothing it out again and again. Providing a box with a single entry cut into it and filled with hay or dirt (if you don't mind) will also keep those who favour digging happy. Many offer their little excavators old phone-directories, newspapers and cardboard.

We have a carpet tube, that the local carpet fitters allowed us to have that Bunny sits either end of and shreds to infinite tiny pieces as well as a carpet tile of her own that we have placed on top of a ruined piece of our carpet to reduce the recreational destruction. Be careful however that Bunny doesn't ingest too much shredded cardboard, paper or carpet fibres as it can block their digestive tract, which in turn can prove fatal. Make sure you are supervising Bunny during their playtimes and keep an eye on their droppings and urine for normality and make sure they are eating and drinking as normal too- you'll soon know if something is wrong.

DROPPINGS
Round, relatively dry, firm droppings that you will see a lot of, usually when Bunny is eating
see also...
Cecotropes p.22
Eliminating p.25
Leaving droppings inside cage p.30
Leaving droppings outside of cage p.31
Signs of illness or injury #2, 5, 6, 7, 10, 11, 12 (p.42)

Simply- Basic rabbit poo.

Bumph- Whilst eating, rabbits will simultaneously eliminate these round firm droppings naturally. There isn't anything wrong with Bunny, it is just how their digestive system works. Some half-digested food is passed seemingly as it is eaten, and some is back-tracked into the cecum to produce the cecotropes a bit later on. These firmer faeces are not re-ingested, although occasionally Bunny may have a nibble. They are eliminated as waste and facilitate the smooth operation of the digestive tract. They are required to keep it in constant motion so the bacteria in the cecum is kept happy and healthy and the tract remains well hydrated.

Droppings are little windows into your Bunny's health. Keep an eye on how much Bunny is eating and drinking and the form, consistency and frequency of their droppings. It sounds like an odd conscious effort to be making but after a week of doing it you will find it's no more a conscious effort then it is a normal observation you make whilst saying 'Good Morning' to Bunny and changing their water.

E is for...

ELIMINATING
The excretion of faecal matter and urinary waste
see also...
Cecotropes p.22
Droppings p.24
Leaving droppings inside cage p.30
Leaving droppings outside of cage p.31
Signs of illness or injury #2, 5, 6, 7, 10, 11, 12 (p.42)

Simply- Bunny's poo and wee- keep a close eye on it. It's a good indicator of Bunny's digestive and overall health.

Bumph - Eliminating is one of the main things a lagomorph owners has issues with. Litter training Bunny really isn't as hard as you think. Our Bunny has pretty much trained herself. She is currently 5 months old, we have had her for just under those 5 months and in that time she has chosen one corner to utilise as a toilet, we placed a litter tray there and Bunny reliably returns there to urinate time and time again even with her cage being accessible by a ramp (it's on top of a short unit). Some rabbits will require more time and patience but generally speaking Bunny will pick a corner and stick to it. Such hygienic and habitual little things.

It is important to become familiar with general elimination, territory markings, stress related markings and litter training mishaps. Each occur for a different reason and each will, if necessary, need to be tackled differently. Keep an eye on how much Bunny is eating and drinking and the form, consistency and frequency of their droppings. It sounds like an odd conscious effort to be making but after a week of doing it you will find it's no more a conscious effort then it is a normal observation you make whilst saying 'Good morning' to Bunny and changing their water... deja vous.

EARS AS HEATERS
How Bunny behaves when they get too cold or too warm.
see also...
The Stress Factor List p.47
Activity p.19
Signs of illness or injury #3, 4, 7, 9 (p.43)

Simply - If Bunny is too hot they will flop out trying to cool off. If Bunny is too cold they will huddle up to keep warm.

Bumph - 45-75 degrees Farenheit or 7-23 degrees Celcius. These are the temperatures a Bunny is most comfortable at. The higher the temperature the more listless and dehydrated your rabbit will become. Unable to sweat or pant like many other animals rabbits are susceptible to brain damage, neurological stresses, strokes and sadly death, as a result of high temperatures.

In a natural setting with Bunny-comfy temperatures they use their ears to moderate their temperature, using the surface area to cool themselves down when getting a little too warm. If it is too cold Bunny's nervous system will be stressed and they will become more susceptible to illnesses, they will not be able to warm themselves up to a more comfortable body temperature and can even freeze to death. In either extremes, measures must be made to make Bunny as comfortable as possible.
▶ Keep them cool without causing a draft,

▶ Keeping them warm without cutting off any ventilation
▶ Provide fresh, not frozen water and clean, fresh foods
▶ Keep their environment, bedding and run area clean and dry and make sure Bunny has a means of snuggling down to keep the chill off or flopping out and keeping cool.

F is for...

FORAGING
Bunny is Rummaging aRound in theiR food bowl and hay

Simply- Bunny is digging about for the best bits of food

Bumph- Bunny instinctively knows they need a lot of fibre. However not being in the wild they have little to no control over what they eat. It is all in your hands. When you provide Bunny with their unlimited supply of hay Bunny will dig through it looking for the tastiest, richest, more preferable blades and cuttings. As far as nuggety-dry foods come into this it is ridiculously important that you shop with Bunny in mind, not your consumer aesthetic tastes. The pretty and colourful mixed bags you see in most pet stores are not nutritionally balanced and encourage selective eating by Bunny. This means Bunny will only eat the bits they like the most and leave the rest; and having a sweet tooth Bunny will more than likely favour the sugary elements over anything else. This is not a well balanced diet and will leave Bunny deficient in vital fibre, minerals and vitamins. In turn this will upset their digestive tract, upset the delicate flora and bacteria in the cecum and lead to an unhealthy, unhappy rabbit.

After Bunny reaches around 7 months nuggets should start to be reduced with fibrous hay becoming the mainstay of Bunny's diet. They can then enjoy foraging for the foods that will keep them fit and healthy and their gut ticking over. A lack of fibre will lead to malocclusions (over grown teeth) and a slowing of the gut's motion. This in turn can cause blockages as the system fails to work correctly.

Blockages are indicated by the sudden lack of faeces or reduction in their normal size. Bunny will also eat and drink less as the blockage slows the tract movement making them feel full, this causes the tract to pull fluids from the system and blockage itself leading to dehydration. There may also be pain or stomach tenderness caused by swelling as gasses from the unbalancing cecum bacteria are produced. Remember to check their droppings and urine for normality regardless of what they are munching on and make sure they are eating and drinking as normal too.

FUR PULLING
Bunny is pulling theiR fuR out!
see also...
The Stress Factor list p.47

Simply- If Bunny is female and it is breeding time then they are nesting and want a fluffy warm nest. If Bunny isn't female or it isn't breeding season then Bunny is stressed, unhappy and possibly ill.

Bumph - There are a few reasons as to why a rabbit, male or female, would actively pull their own fur out. Female fur pulling from the dewlap (the big fluffy mass on the chest) is instinctively a nesting behaviour, lining the nest with her own fur to keep the impending kits safe and warm.

▶ If a spayed/ neutered male and female pair are bonded then stress, mites, mange, other skin conditions or boredom can cause either to pull fur out.
▶ If neither are spayed or neutered it could be a true pregnancy.
▶ If only the female is spayed then the female fur pulling could be due to stress from the sex-pest male.
▶ False pregnancy in lone unspayed females will also initiate nesting behaviour.

It will depend greatly on the inclusion or absence of another rabbit, whether or not they're spayed/ neutered, stresses in the environment and whether or not it is possible for an illness or injury to be factored in. With the exclusion of it being a spayed lone female with no signs of illness or injury, a visit to a rabbit-savvy vet will be in order, to book spay/ neuter surgery, be looked over for underlying medical conditions and make sure the fur pulling hasn't caused any serious skin damage,

FLOPPING
Bunny suddenly falls on their side
See also...
Signs of illness or injury #9 (p.42)

Simply- Your rabbit has reached destination Nirvana.

Bumph- A contented, happy, healthy, safe and loved Bunny is a floppy Bunny. This behaviour really does make you panic the first few times you witness it. Bunny acts as if they have suddenly dropped dead (for lack of a better term). You spend a few seconds staring at Bunny wondering what is going on and only start to breathe again when they fidget or get back up. The times our Bunny has worried me in this manner; I'm glad she's happy but couldn't rabbits express it in a less alarming way?

FLICKING FEET
Bunny hopped off flicking their back feet
see also...
Temper tantrums p.37

Simply- The lagomorph equivalent of giving you the two-fingers.

Bumph- When you have severely annoyed, denigrated or insulted Bunny you can expect to be given the foot flick. This comes before being completely shut out by Bunny as they compact themselves into a flattened bread-loaf type form. Rabbits hold grudges quite well. Never mind that an elephant never forgets, rabbits let you off then bring it back up again later. It takes many treats, fuss, play and attention to get rabbit-forgiveness and even then it is on their term. Beware the Bunny-grudge!

G is for...

GROOMING
Bunny spends ages licking their paws and washing themselves
see also...
Licking p.29
Signs of illness or injury #16 (p.42)

Simply- Rabbits are highly meticulous groomers and spend hours making themselves pristine.

Bumph- Rabbits groom themselves and each other as part of bonding and socialising. It helps maintain the top Bunnys' dominance and also makes the shedding process more efficient. Bunnies moult every 3 ish months with heavier moults following lighter moults. For this reason Bunny will need to groom quite fastidiously to help the old coat shed quickly. Grooming your rabbit during the heavier moults is pretty much obligatory. Just like cats, rabbits can and do get hair-balls. Hair-balls in a Bunny is not good as they have extreme difficulties passing it and any digestive blockage is a countdown to fatality for a Bunny. This is because unlike cats, a rabbit is physically unable to vomit so the hair-ball has only one direction to go. In the event of a digestive blockage, veterinary intervention is a must as poorly rabbits degenerate within hours.

Blockages are indicated by the sudden lack of faeces or reduction in their normal size. Bunny will also eat and drink less as the blockage slows the tract movement making them feel full, this causes the tract to pull fluids from the system and blockage itself leading to dehydration. There may also be pain or stomach tenderness caused by swelling as gasses, from the unbalancing cecum bacteria, are produced. Make sure you check their droppings and urine for normality and make sure they are eating and drinking as normal too during moults.

GRUNTING
Bunny keeps making grunting sort of growly sounds at me
see also...
The Stress Factor List p.47
Aggressive Behaviour p.18
Temper Tantrums p.37
Noises p.32
Signs of illness or injury #1, 2, 13, 15 (p.42)

Simply- This is Bunny's way of saying "Get lost and leave me alone NOW"

Bumph- It's likely you have really annoyed Bunny or are doing something that consistently irks them. Consider this grunting your verbal warning. It is a clear expression that you are starting to get on Bunny's nerves and need to go away and let them be. You may be trying to pick them up, interrupting their fun, waking them up rudely, invading their home, hurting them or they may be in pain from illness and injury and your actions are making the discomfort worse. Leave Bunny alone for the time being and wait for them to come to you.

Try to back-track what has occurred leading up to the grunting. When you've ascertained what it initiated the behaviour try to approach it from a different angle (if necessary) a little bit later- you don't want to stress Bunny out any more, less you want to get bitten. If you suspect illness or injury then try to keep an eye on their droppings and urine for normality and make sure they are eating and drinking as normal too, contact your rabbit-savvy vet and get Bunny checked over.

H

I

J

K is for...

KICKING OUT

Bunny thrashes about and kicks out when I pick them up

see also...
Aggressive behaviour p.18
Signs of illness or injury #1 (p.42)

Simply- Bunnies don't like being picked up. Put them down and leave them alone for a bit.

Bumph- Rabbits are prey animals, they are built to run away- they cannot do this 5ft off the ground. Being able to pick up and cuddle your Bunny is something many owners are eager to do but to a rabbit it is no different to being captured by a predator. Being caught and restrained is terrifying to Bunny regardless of how strong your bond with them is. Just because they trust and love you on ground level does not mean it will be the same in the air. There is nothing you can do to change Bunny's mind on this one. It is hardwired into their brain. Some rabbits tolerate it, most despise it.

Instead try to appreciate the ability to sit on the sofa and have Bunny snuggle by your side, or on your lap, or just sitting with Bunny on the floor. Forcing Bunny to endure something that panics them will only cause Bunny to be stressed which can lead to stress related health complications and undesirable aggression towards you. If you need to hold Bunny for nail trimming, vet visits, ear checks or giving medicine etc then make sure you learn how to pick up and hold Bunny properly. They have very fragile skeletal structures and their bones can break easily, it will also save your arm being shredded.

L is for...

LICKING

Bunny licks you, your clothes or around you

see also...
Grooming p.28
Flopping p.27
Tooth purrs p.36
Binkying p.19

Simply- If the licks are accompanied with nibbles you are being groomed! If they are just licks you technically are getting Bunny kisses. Bunny loves you.

Bumph- If your rabbit is healthy, happy, comfortable and well socalised then they are likely to express how ecstatic their life is in many ways, running the Bunny 500, binkying, flopping, tooth purrs, grooming you and giving sweet little Bunny kisses (little tickly licks).

Bunny's grooming instinct can be initiated by you already stroking them, they will then in turn offer to groom you. If you have a particularly affectionate Bunny they will just start licking and grooming you as they please.

My fellow human and I (and some plush chickens) are regularly groomed and licked. My hands, the chicken's heads and beaks and fellow human's clothes are all accustomed to being in contact with Bunny's tongue. With the clothes-licking it is merely Bunny not being 100% sure where you start and the clothes finish. It's just your coat of fur as far as Bunny is concerned. My hands get kisses and groomed. Grooming is made obvious by Bunny gently nibbling fingertips and nails as if grooming the fur on another rabbit. Bunny doesn't realise that the nibbling can hurt a little. The plush chickens... well they are just filthy, obviously, as they get groomed every single day, sometimes twice. If your Bunny doesn't seem like they are up to much licking then do not worry. Some bunnies can't help themselves and others just aren't all that fussed about showing you any 'lurve' - they are there to be respected and waited on hand and foot, they cannot be expected to be dominant and dote on you now can they?

LAYING FULL LENGHT
Bunny lays full length with back legs stretched out underneath them

Simply- *You have a very chilled, content and safe feeling Bunny splashed out on your floor.*

Bumph- Being a prey animal rabbits generally prefer to sit in corners, under tables, or in strategically safe places that allow Bunny to keep an eye on things whilst happy that things aren't creeping up on them. A very trusting and happy Bunny will lie full length to relax and doze, secure in the knowledge that although they are vulnerable in that position they will come to no harm. This is most likely to be seen when the day's chaos has come to an end and it's calm and quiet in the room with nothing to alarm or keep Bunny on their anti-predator toes.

LEAVING DROPPINGS IN CAGE
Bunny is leaving droppings all over their cage floor!

see also...
Droppings p.24
Cecotropes p.22
Elimination p.25
Leaving droppings outside of the cage p.31
The Stress Factor List p.47
Signs of illness or injury #2, 5, 6, 7, 10, 11, 12 (p.42)

Simply- Bunny is establishing their new cage as theirs or Bunny is marking their cage again because of an environmental stress factor.

Bumph- When you get a new Bunny and introduce it to its new home they will begin establishing what is theirs. Their space, safe haven, their bed and their litter tray, sometimes even their food bowl. To do this they will seemingly just leave pellets all over the cage floor. This isn't the same as eating and simultaneously eliminating nor is it a litter training mishap. They are in fact just mass marking their private, exclusive space. If you do a bit of 'Googling' about the matter some people will comment that this is not territorial marking- that they use their stronger smelling urine for that, but there is a difference between marking territory and marking out your private space when you just move into it.

After a few days when Bunny is content that the area is theirs and all safe and sound they will stop randomly leaving pellets everywhere. Excessive cleaning of the cage by humans, too much space too soon, stress, introduction of a new family member/ rabbit or not feeling safe and secure at any time may kick start this means of marking again. Generally the pellets are dry and odorless so fear not! A quick vacuum will sort it out if the 'markings' escape outside of the cage. Happy contented and secure bunnies will seldom do it- the odd accident may occur but otherwise the poop-a-lot sesson should soon stop. Once it has cleared up and no longer looks like a giant litter tray with a rabbit in it, be considerate to Bunny and their natural instincts:

▶ Do not force them in or out of their safe place.
▶ Let them come to you & usher them back in, don't place them back in.
▶ Do not make their safe place a form of punishment or prison.
▶ Try to clean it and change food/ water when Bunny isn't in there.

LEAVING DROPPINGS OUTSIDE OF CAGE
Bunny keeps leaving droppings everywhere outside of their cage

see also...
Droppings p.24
Cecotropes p.22
Elimination p.25
Leaving droppings inside the cage p.30
The Stress Factor List p.47
Signs of illness or injury #2, 5, 6, 7, 10, 11, 12 (p.42)

Simply- Bunny is unhappy about something, is in pain or ill, is a hormonal teen, is too little to know or you've given them too much space too soon and they've forgotten where their toilet is.

Bumph- If your Bunny appears to be happily settled in their little place yet pellets keep appearing all over the shop take into account the Bunny's age and absolutely anything that could cause Bunny to be stressed.

▶ 8 weeks - 14 weeks they are still babies and generally speaking don't know what their bladder/ bowel is doing or why. They will not take easily to training because they are just so young and won't be able to make the connection between something they don't understand and something you want them to do.
▶ 14 weeks + (the teenage .years') will be litter training hell due to hormones. Scenting and marking territory is all they have on the brain- just smells, smells, smells. Never mind not understanding their own bowels etc they just want to get as much of them around as much as they can. Once neutered or spayed and resettled they will be more receptive to their litter tray training.
▶1 year and beyond (reliable adults) will be much easier to train to use their tray for both urination and defecation so any abnormal leaving of droppings may be due to stress factors or illness.

Anything from moving furniture, loud noises, pain, lack of socialising- literally anything that changes something in their routine or environment can cause Bunny to express displeasure by simply leaving pellets outside of the cage. Bunny may have been given too much room to play in too quickly and it's all a little bit overwhelming. Limit the space and let them re-familiarise themselves with their exclusive room again. Slowly expand the play area over a matter of weeks so Bunny can re-orientate themselves. Too much space too soon could suggest to Bunny that their cage and all this is new room is theirs; you need Bunny to understand what space is theirs and what is yours. The odd accident will always occur, normally just the odd random pellet or three that has materialised seemingly from nowhere but aside that, as long as no routines are dramatically upset and no stresses introduced, it should be as you desire.

LUNGING

Bunny jumped at me and bit me

see also...
Aggressive behaviour p.18
Biting p.20
The Stress Factor List p.47
Signs of illness or injury #1 (p.42)

Simply- You may have ignored a few prior warnings and this was the consequence, if not then you really made Bunny mad.

Bumph- Bunny was either instantly riled or you didn't get the memo. Lunging is normally accompanied with ears pressed flat against Bunny's back and rapid repositioning to launch and a bite. This is Bunny's subtle way of saying "Back right off and never do that again". It's a last resort for something that has been bugging them for a while or an instant 3 strikes with the added note that repeats will not be tolerated. Whatever initiated this behaviour it needs to be addressed immediately.

Back-track and define what it was that caused Bunny to react this way. Also take into account that it isn't aggression (per se) it is Bunny's reaction to fear of something horrible happening to them. When you figure out what initiated the response, find a means of approaching it from another direction if necessary or simply never do it again. You may find Bunny to be a bit .off' with you afterwards. Just let them calm down and relax before trying to interact with them again and don't be offended. Bunny still loves you, you just shook them up a little.

M

N is for...

NOISES

Bunny is making strange noises

see also...
Thumping p.38
Tooth purrs p.36
Signs of illness or injury #13 (p.42)

Simply- Bunny can make 5 main noises. The most common noises heard are honks, grunts, squeals, tooth purrs and loud tooth grinding; 6 noises if you include foot thumps.

Bumph- Rabbits are only 'mostly' silent. But for what it's worth lagomorphs can produce 5 noises (6 with the thumping). These noises aren't very loud in themselves bar the squeals or shrill screams which I sincerely hope you never ever hear. Different variations of pitch or tone will be heard depending on the Bunny with grunts crossing with growls or sounding more like hisses, honks sounding more like coos and the occasional squeak that I have yet to hear myself.

Honking sounds like a tiny, tiny goose slowly loosing its voice. Honking/ cooing is a happy sound and one also made by kits when communicating with their mother. Grunting sounds like short little growls and are quite gruff. Depending on the context they can be associated with the mating feet circling, can mean "Stop that and go away" or a less threatening "Not today pesky human". Tooth purrs are tiny vibrations of Bunny's teeth knocking together and means they are happy and contented. Soft and gentle stroking of Bunny's ears, cheeks (if they like it) and back can elicit happy little tooth purrs. More distinctive and louder tooth grinding is indicative of pain or discomfort and something your rabbit-savvy vet should investigate. The squeals or screams are also indicative of extreme pain and being helplessly terrified.

NIPPING
Bunny keeps nipping me
see also...
Grooming p.28
Nudging p.33
Signs of illness or injury #1 (p.42)

Simply- You might be annoying Bunny, pestering them, be in their way or not giving them the attention they think they deserve at that precise second in time.

Bumph- Nips can mean a variety of things. Our little ball of fluff nips and digs at the bottom of my trouser legs if they are in her way (as walking around my feet is totally out of the question). Nips also occur during a good hearty grooming session. Your rabbit doesn't understand that the nips occasionally hurt and they are not done with the intent of causing harm. Even the nips of annoyance, which are more like a human variation of a 'clip around the ear', are not meant to hurt.

If you stop Bunny doing something interesting, invade their exclusively-Bunny-only cage or take something they are happily chewing off of them you may get an irritated nip, if Bunny is feeling rather amorous your ankles may also get nipped during a bit of foot circling. If it really did hurt then a short sharp squeal will communicate to Bunny that they were a little too hard on you, nothing too loud or dramatic though or you'll end up with another nip for making Bunny jump.

NUDGING
Bunny keeps pushing my hand away with their nose
see also...
Grooming p.28
Nudging p.33

Simply- Bunny wants you to stroke or groom them, wants your attention or is begging for treats... or yet again you are in the way.

Bumph- If you are busy and Bunny's attempts of communicating their desire to be lavished upon go unheard you may find your hand being nudged as a final ditch attempt to get your attention. Bunny doesn't want to be too forceful, as they know they won't get the treat or stroke if they nip you on this occasion. You may also just be in the way, again, but Bunny is feeling pretty chipper and is just happily suggesting that you move the obstacle.

Begging is also expressed by Bunny attempting to climb your legs if you are seated, nudging your hands or feet and leaning on you if standing, the little honking sort of cooing noises are sometimes used as well- the method will vary rabbit to rabbit. Don't ignore them for too long though or your skirting boards will go missing.

NIBBLING YOUR HAIR
It's so sweet, Bunny keeps eating my hair
see also...
Grooming p.28

Simply- Yes it's cute but do not allow it. It is bad for Bunny's digestive tract.

Bumph- Although cute and initially funny, this is a humongously massive big 'no no' (NB: 'Humongously' is not an actual word).

Human hair, regardless of length, is bad for a rabbit's digestive tract. It can and will cause blockages, digestive complications, get tangled up inside the tract and all sorts of other nasty and intricately disastrous things. Rabbits have issues with their own hair and hair-balls let alone having to try and deal with issues caused by ingesting our Human hair. Hair up or pinned back or wear a hat- shave it all off if you must just do not let your Bunny snack on your hair. They might be attempting to groom you, just testing to see what it is, genuinely be eating it or just be chewing on it like it's the skirting board. Whatever the reason it is not remotely beneficial for them to do it and you mustn't allow it. Unless of course you are a dab hand at rabbit keyhole surgery.

O

P is for...

PERISCOPING
Bunny Raises themselves up onto their hind legs and scopes the enviRonment

Simply- Bunny is checking out the vicinity either for potential threats, because something sparked their attention or just to be nosey

Bumph- This is your prey animal's way of gaining some height to get a better view of their surroundings. Rabbits love climbing and often perch on top of boxes, the sofa, shoulders and anything else they can comfortably get on and off of as the height advantage allows them a superior view of the environment than that of when they are on the ground. Bunny will raise themselves up onto their hind legs; lift their chins and even attempt standing on their tip toes before loosing balance... in a controlled and demure fashion of course.

Q

R is for...

RESTING
Bunny seems to be sitting and doing nothing

see also...
Activity p.19
Sleeping with eyes open p.35
Signs of illness or injury #3, 4 (p.42)

Simply- Your rabbit is just sitting and having some down time.

Bumph- Rabbits are on guard all day long and need to catch some down time eventually. Rabbits will snooze, doze, chill out, flop and just sit at random intervals through out the day. The frequency will vary from day to day depending on Bunny's mood. Rabbits rest in a variety of ways. They will sit comfortably with their hind legs underneath and front paws tucked under their chest. Ears will be alert but Bunny will be half-zoned out. They will lie full length, relax their normal sitting position a little and not be so compact or just flop to the side and recline in the lap of luxury.

S is for...

SITTING UNDER TABLES/ IN CORNERS
Bunny spends a lot of time sitting under the table or in a box

see also...
Laying full length p.30
Signs of illness or injury #3, 4 (p.42)

Simply- Sitting under cover reduces their vulnerability to predators.

Bumph- Sitting in such a strategic matter is one of Bunny's natural anti-predation behaviours. Nothing can creep up on you if there is no room to do so and with the view left wide open for Bunny to keep an eye on things they can ensure that danger isn't advancing upon them. Bunny may alternate between flopping on the sofa, to sitting in a box to sleeping under a chair as and when the fancy takes them. It might also be more comfortable to doze under the table where there is shading from light. Bunny may also just be keeping out of the way if you have annoyed them, they feel too much is going on elsewhere or they just want some space to themselves without having to return to their cage.

SLEEPING WITH EYES OPEN
Is the Rabbit asleep? I can't tell their eyes are open...

Simply- You cannot keep an eye on things when they are closed.

Bumph- Another anti-predation action. Catching some Z's with their eyes open means Bunny can get some rest whilst allowing any sudden movements to instantly alert them to potential threats. Bunny will sleep with their eyes closed when tucked up all safe and sound or when they feel completely safe and at ease. However if you still aren't sure if Bunny is sleeping or just staring into space then check their little noses for movements. When a Bunny is sound asleep their nose will stop its constant twitching. Their ears will also be relaxed and laid flat as opposed to upright and waiting to detect sounds that may indicate danger.

SPRAYING URINE
Bunny just flicked wee at me!

see also...
Chin rubbing p.22
Urinating on the bed/ chair p.38
The Stress Factor List p.47
Signs of illness or injury #2, 5, 6, 7, 10, 11, 12 (p.42)

Simply- Male Bunny, who isn't neutered, is in the mood for 'lurve', Bunny is marking their territory casually or as a result of environmental stresses or Bunny may have a urinary tract infection.

Bumph- Both male and female rabbits will mark territory with urine. It is strong smelling and other animals will get the hint very quickly. The marking does not necessarily have to be sprayed however and not every rabbit will do it to the same extent. Our little Bunny has yet to be spayed and just urinates plain and simple, no elaborate flare or spraying, just sits, raises her backside and tail and urinates, she doesn't do it that often either. Intact males are more likely to spray however and neutering will help reduce if not stop this behaviour. The fact you got sprayed is just unfortunate. Bunny now owns you.

Spraying is an extension of chin rubbing and the raging hormones from hitting maturity make the need to scent mark even more intense for them. Book Bunny in for spay or neuter surgery at your rabbit-savvy vets and the spraying will cease. If Bunny is already spayed or neutered then the behaviour could lend to environmental stresses that result in Bunny feeling the need to stake claim to certain areas or it is indicative of illness/ injury. Again a visit to the rabbit-savvy vet will be necessary to be checked over and treated if there is a complication.

T is for...

TOOH PURRS
Bunny is making a strange little sound and their head is sort of... vibrating
See also

Signs of illness or injury #1, 13 (p.42)

Simply - Bunny is very happy and to show it they are purring, rabbit style.

Bumph- When happy or in the receipt of a pleasurable stroking session Bunny will rapidly chatter their teeth together which produces a tooth-purr. This chattering feels like a small vibration radiating from Bunny's jaw or head and can vary from a gentle movement, to an audible chattering noise. It can also sound like they are munching nuggets but do not mistake it for loud tooth grinding that is indicative of pain and discomfort. If it is more grinding then chattering then check Bunny's body language for tensing and signs of pain related behaviour, keep an eye on their eliminations, eating and drinking and seek advice from a rabbit-savvy vet.

TANTRUMS

Bunny appears to be in a bad mood today

see also...
Aggressive behaviour p.18
The Stress Factor list p.47
Signs of illness or injury #1 (p.42)

Simply- Just like you and I Bunny will have an 'off' day, will be annoyed or angered by something and will seemingly go out of their way to express it.

Bumph- If Bunny seems to be expressing aggressive behaviour but you really haven't done anything yet then Bunny could quite simply just be having a moody day, hour or just a little temper tantrum session. Our Bunny throws her toys about, grunts and growls at everything, won't present herself for grooming or strokes and generally stays away from you; normally because she wasn't let out to play at the usual time or because we didn't greet her on getting up. Rabbits are well known for their little temper tantrums and it is just part and parcel of having a big personality in a small being.

They have rubbish moods and days just like us and it is best to just let them get on with it. If you can back-track or decipher the riddle of what caused today's behaviour then go for it- take into account any environmental stresses, dietary changes or changes in routine and just sit back and causally observe. It could be that Bunny is coming down with something and that a closer eye needs to be kept on them.

If the behaviour is infrequent or a one off then Bunny was just being a bit of a Diva. If it's becoming somewhat of a habit then you will need to get your investigative hat on and keep the rabbit-savvy vet's number close to hand incase medical intervention is required. In the mean time, let Bunny be Bunny and keep monitoring their eliminations for normality and make sure they are eating and drinking as normal too. Their mood will pick up soon and the strokes may commence once again.

TIP-TOEING

Bunny is tip-toeing carefully around things

Simply- Bunny is investigating something new and is approaching it with caution.

Bumph- Rabbits walk on their toes anyway, whereas we mooch about on the flat soles of our feet. When something new is introduced to the home, a new toy, new piece of furniture or if you are offering Bunny some food they haven't recognised yet then they will tip-toe up to it or elongate their body's towards it in a sort of tip-toe-stretch before assessing. When happy that the new thing is safe they will relax and bring their body nearer to investigate more thoroughly. This cautious approach allows Bunny to jump back hastily if necessary and allows them to twist their body to run if they are startled or threatened by the new object.

THUMPING
Bunny makes a loud thumping noise with their feet

See also...
Noises p.32

Simply- "Danger Will Robison. Danger."

Bumph- If Bunny hears, smells or sees impending danger they will sound the alarm so everyone in the herd can retreat to the warren, run for cover or help periscope for the potential threat. This is a social anti-predation behaviour that allows Bunny to protect themselves on both individual and group levels. The group can happily go about their day's activities knowing that at least one of them will pick up on potential threats. After all several pairs of eyes, noses and ears are better than one.

The sound is unmistakable and can be performed with either foot singly or both simultaneously, Bunny may also perform the thumping in situ or whilst running for safety. The thump replicates a rather meaty sounding rabbit-sized thunderclap. It is made by Bunny hitting the flooring with the flat of their hind feet.

Some rabbits use it as a general display of anger, upset or disapproval, some are quite thumpy and some are more laid back and sure of their surroundings. Pay attention to any changes or occurrences that could be causing frequent thumping and address as necessary- Bunny may be stressed over something and we most certainly cannot have that.

U is for...

URINATING ON BED/ CHAIRS
Bunny keeps weeing on the chair or bed

see also...
Spraying urine p.38
Chin rubbing p.22
The Stress Factor list p.47
Signs of illness or injury #2, 5, 6, 7, 10, 11, 12 (p.42)

Simply- Bunny is behaving in accordance to hormones, dominance and territory marking exercises, Bunny may also be stressed or ill.

Bumph- Constant or repeat urinating on beds and chairs is a result of it being warm, 'squidgy', a large area, nice and absorbent like their litter tray and more importantly- it will smell to high heaven (to a rabbit's sensitive nose) of you. And Bunny really cannot have that.
Because you've gone to all the effort of marking it for yourself Bunny will need to:

▶ Mark it as their territory in the first instance
▶ Remind you that it is theirs, if marked already at a previous time
▶ Cover your smell up with theirs, because your smell is over powering their previous reminder
▶ Add their smell to yours for the good of the herd!

Living with more than one being constitutes as living in a herd. In a herd there are hierarchies; like a social ladder of dominance. Bunny needs to establish where on this ladder everyone in the herd is. Like most animals Bunny wants to be at the top and being at the top means they own everything, they own you, they own the bed, the chair, whatever it is they are urinating on.

Scent marking with a massive puddle of Bunny-wee will communicate this perfectly. Perfectly to them anyway, not so ideal for us- although you do get the message. It's hard not to really.

Alternatively if Bunny is spayed/ neutered and the behaviour is new then it could relate to either a new environmental stress factor or illness. Take into account Bunny's age as well. Older rabbits have a hard time using their litter trays and adaptations will need to be made to compensate. Old or ill rabbits may also have weakened bladders or be in too much pain or discomfort to get to the litter tray. Young rabbits are either a rage of hormones and spay or neutering will sort it out or they are too little to understand the function of their bladder and you'll just have to be patient. If concerned and other signs or symptoms of illness present themselves then seek advice from your rabbit-savvy vet.

V

W is for...

WATCHING T.V
Is Bunny actually watching this Rubbish?

Simply- Yes. Although what exactly Bunny sees is speculative.

Bumph- Bunny's eyes are positioned so they have what is essentially a 360 view of their surroundings, which they can observe without moving their head. This positioning however produces a blind spot right in front of them so anything you present to them face on isn't visually appreciated.

TV's are generally positioned on a piece of furniture or mounted, raising the screen up to a level that Bunny can see above their head. The bright lighting and screen display may also aid Bunny in T.V viewing. Because their eyes have evolved to work efficiently in the twilight hour's light intensity, the bright screen display may be more vivid to Bunny and so more interesting to look at. Bunny's are also thought to be able to see shapes and forms as opposed to the detailed images we see, so when we suggest Bunny is watching T.V they are more observing the shapes whilst chilling out on the sofa as the T.V is part of their environment and the on-screen movement is just an extension of activity that is going on in the surroundings. Bunny is watching T.V in the same manner as watching fellow herd members play chase... all speculation of course but it sounds fair enough to me.

X

Y

Z

A page for scribbles.

6th chapter

- SIGNS OF ILLNESS OR INJURY -

Bunny may not be acting up or behaving differently just because you've had neighbours over and cooked a joint of lamb. It may also be because Bunny isn't well or has hurt themselves. If this is the case then quick medical intervention from your rabbit-savvy vet is an absolute must as poorly rabbits can go down hill very quickly, sometimes in a matter of hours.

SIGNS OF ILLNESS OR INJURY
Bunny's aggressive behaviour may not be due to fear

There is a very long and sad list of illness, conditions, diseases, viruses, bacterial infections and ailments that can strike your rabbit at any given time depending on the condition of their health and well-being, the state of their environment, the quality of their diet and the closeness of your observations.

Inherently because wild rabbits breed so prolifically, when ill they give up the fight very quickly. The species is so numerous they just let nature run her course and keep the natural balance. For this reason and due to the severity of the illnesses, rabbits can die within 24hrs of becoming unwell.

Firstly make sure you get Bunny vaccinated against Myxomatosis and Viral Hemorrhagic Disease. Do this whether Bunny lives outside or in the house.

Secondly when Bunny is old enough (normally around 6 months) make sure you have them neutered. This will save the female developing uterine cancer later in life, reduce destructive behaviour in both sexes as well making life a lot calmer, chilled and for-filling for them.

Thirdly keep a keen eye on their behaviour and make sure any new behaviours or changes in normal ones are looked into. If you've back-tracked events and cannot find an environmental or social cause then the change in behaviour may be because Bunny is ill or injured:

1 Pain and discomfort on being handled
When picked up Bunny displays aggressive behaviour physically or vocally.

Do not assume that Bunny is merely telling you they hate being picked up. They could be experiencing pain or be in discomfort and your handling of them is making it worse.

2 Pain and discomfort on eliminating
Bunny makes audible noises whilst going to the toilet.

Observe Bunny as they urinate or produce droppings. They may be having difficulty passing the waste and straining painfully as a result.

3 Lethargy and listlessness
You Bunny is abnormally idle and lifeless.

Bunny is unlikely to be having an off day and is instead ill; feeling too poorly to do anything and not having the energy to perform their basic grooming or even make it to the litter tray.

4 Not alert
Bunny isn't as reactive or aware of their surrounding

They are slow to react to stimuli and do not appear to be focused or fully awake. Do not mistake a sleeping Bunny for a non-alert Bunny.

5 Not eating as normal or at all
The food bowl is still full and the hay is untouched

Rabbits eat constantly, on a healthy and nutritionally balanced diet they do not get 'stuffed full'. A reduction in appetite should not be taken as Bunny not having room for munchies.

6 Not drinking as normal or not at all
The water crock or bottle is still full

Most of the food you will give Bunny will have a low water content. Bunny will be drinking a fair amount to compensate for this. Bunny should always fancy a drink or two.

7 Drinking more than normal
The water crock or bottle empties quicker than normal

Although your Bunny should be drinking throughout the day excessive drinking is a sign that something is making Bunny dehydrate.

8 Head shaking and shudders
Bunny keeps shaking their head or shuddering

Do not mistake this behaviour for binkies. If it is abnormally frequent and the head shaking is bias to one side then something is wrong.

9 Collapsing
Bunny falls to their sides or fronts with particular weakness in the hind legs

Again do not mistake this for the normal happy flopping behaviour. Bunny is certainly not happy.

10 Urinating more than normal
Bunny is urinating more frequently in and out of litter tray

When a rabbit urinates they really go for it. Do not assume Bunny is marking territory or rebelling against litter training.

11 Mushy unformed droppings
Droppings are being left that are unformed and icky

Smaller than normal, mushy or unformed droppings are not a litter training or territory behavoiur so make sure you do not over look it.

pour l'amour de persil • pour l'amour de persil • pour l'amour de persil • pour l'amour de p

12 Less droppings than normal or none at all
Bunny's litter tray is suddenly very clean

If during your observations you notice little to no droppings or smaller sized ones then something is wrong. Bunny should always be producing firm, round, uniform droppings as part of a healthy digestive system and diet.

13 Noisy breathing
Bunny makes a rasping or snuffly sound when breathing

Do not mistake this as one of Bunny's 5 common noises. Less it is normal for Bunny it is unlikely to be an amorous display of affection or a warning grunt.

14 Walking in circles
You Bunny starts walking around in circles possibly with a tilted head

This behaviour is not to be mistaken with a happy Bunny circling its favourite toys or human and is completely unrelated to the amorous feet-circling.

15 Making noises on rest or when active
Bunny is making noises when normally they are quiet

Bunny may be vocalising pain or discomfort that flares up when they move about or occurs even when at rest.

16 Scratching ears persistently
Bunny is itching their ears a lot

Rabbits groom their ears frequently as part of a whole body-wash. Do not mistake persistent itching as a grooming session or casual itch of their ear.

If Bunny starts displaying any of these behaviours seek advice from your rabbit-savvy vet as soon as possible. If left, a poorly rabbit can die from its condition over night.

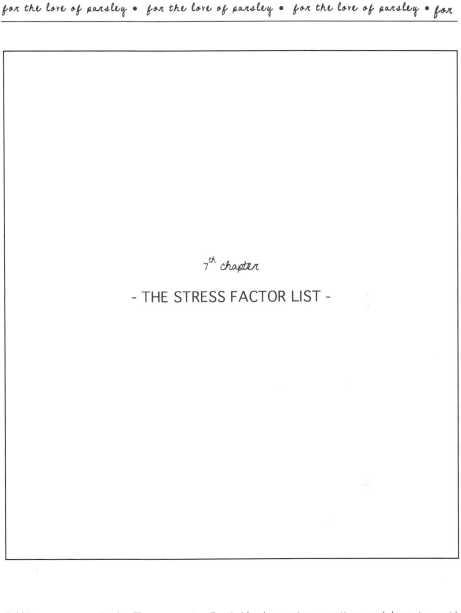

7th chapter

- THE STRESS FACTOR LIST -

Rabbits are prey animals. They are naturally timid, shy, curious, cautious and keen to avoid stressful situations. In the wild they can do this with ease. They have their entire environment at their disposal and have the freedom to control what they can and cannot avoid. Pet rabbits do not have this freedom, so stress and anxiety plays a huge, huge, huge 99.9% roll in behavioural problems. The other .1% are just very expressive characters.

THE STRESS FACTOR
Things that cause bunny to act out of character

If Bunny is doing something less than desirable and it is **out of character for them** then it's likely to be Bunny's way of communicating they are stressing over something. Stress, anxiety, fear, depression, illness and injury will all be communicated if Bunny is experiencing them.

Obviously because bunnies cannot communicate on a human level they show us they are unhappy in a good number of other ways- some methods are by far less-than-subtle. Neon signs would be more subtle...

(Behavioural) Generally they may show you by **out of character** behaviours such as...

▶ Urinating and leaving droppings everywhere

▶ Digging in or at things they normally ignore

▶ Chewing on things they normally ignore

▶ Not eating or drinking as normal

▶ Unformed droppings/ mushy droppings

▶ Producing night time droppings and not eating them

▶ Hiding or attempting to escape

▶ Grooming a lot more than normal

▶ Pulling out furr

(Emotional) and when you try to interact with them...

▶ Being overly jumpy

▶ Being lethargic and unresponsive or uninterested

▶ Ears laid back tightly

▶ Squeaking or vocalising

▶ Flinching when you go to touch them

▶ Biting you

▶ Having a tense body

▶ Nudging and pushing your hand away

The above examples are representative of just a few means of showing you there is something wrong. Generally speaking, if Bunny is doing something odd that they **do not normally do and it is sudden** then they are showing you something is not right. Finding out what exactly is wrong is where the detective work comes in. It can be something so small and insignificant to us that we don't even realise it or it can be something rather obvious but we over look it.

THE LIST

Here is a, by no means exhaustive, list compiled from goodness knows how many sources of stress/ anxiety/ depressive stimuli that may upset your Bunnykins:

▶ Loud noises

▶ Traveling in a car

▶ Heat

▶ Cold

▶ Illness

▶ Moving house

▶ Cage being cleaned out

▶ Food they do not like

▶ Not enough food

▶ Overcrowding

▶ Boredom from lack of toys

▶ Not being able to express natural behaviour

▶ Lack of socializing

▶ Lack of exercise

▶ Pain

▶ Other pets (dogs, cats, birds etc)

▶ Other pets they see as predators

▶ A companion rabbit that is too dominant

▶ A new companion rabbit being introduced

▶ Any other new pet being introduced

▶ Being handled badly and anticipating it

▶ Unfamiliar environments

▶ Too much or too little light

▶ Stale water

▶ A New cage

▶ Items in cage being moved about

▶ New items of furniture

▶ Furniture being moved around

▶ Visitors to your house

▶ New/ unfamiliar smells

▶ Fireworks

▶ Too small a cage

▶ Change of daily routine

▶ The smell of cooking

▶ The smell of cooked meats

▶ Intact Males harassing spayed females

▶ Being hormonal and not spayed/ neutuered

▶ Being constantly harrassed

Most of the above are what is considered as a 'novelty event'. It is either a one off and things will quickly return as they were or they occur and Bunny just has to learn to get use to it and settle back into their routines, which now include this 'new' occurrence.

The aggressive or undesirable behaviour will need addressing as soon as possible. Reverse the environmental change or stress and Bunny will settle back into their normal routines happy and confident that the thing upsetting them has gone. If it cannot be reversed, removed or changed then you will have to work with Bunny in building a new routine and getting them used to the change.

Things like cooking, having visitors over or traveling in a car are short-lived events and you should just make sure that Bunny is as comfortable as can be for the duration. Normally once the stimuli are removed Bunny will return to their normal little selves.

Sometimes it can take a good few days to a week for Bunny to settle back down, depending on the environmental stress and how they reacted to it.

KEEPING A BUNNY DIARY
Keep track of what you change incase it causes Bunny stress

We have kept a diary since we move our Bunny in giving us a base of normality to work from if she does start acting out of character. We use it to record any changes or events that we facilitate that could cause Bunny to react. This helps us understand her dislikes and reactions to them and if necessary allows the vet to see what has recently occurred to aid in any diagnosis.

We record all changes in food (new foods being introduced or being taken away), significant changes in playtime durations, if we've not been around as much as usual or if Bunny was caught red-handed eating carpet fibres or too much cardboard etc.

If all this seems like hard work, a little bit unnecessary and time consuming we can assure you it isn't. It very quickly becomes second nature and doesn't take more than a couple of minutes. Bunny quickly becomes part of the family and falls into your in-home routine. You end up doing it without thinking.

Diligence and observation is also a lot, lot cheaper than a vet bill!

> **18th February 2011**
>
> Morgs is eating + drinking as normal.
> Droppings are normal
> urine is chalky white again
>
> we introduced her to carrot today. Wasn't that fussed about it.
>
> cleared cage out too.

> **24th February 2011**
>
> Morgs wasn't let out for long today. Seems a bit stressy.
>
> droppings are normal
> urine is back to normal
> eating and drinking is good
>
> try and let her out for longer tomorrow.

(scan of our diary)

a page for scribbles.

A page for scribbles.

INDEX OF BEHAVIOURS

chapter number - page number

Thank you!

Many thanks to those who gave up their precious time to review this guide, thanks to Dan for putting up with my manic work ethic and bunny-madness, thanks to Morgs for not eating the entire skirting-board whilst my back was turned and an even bigger thank you to you for buying this guide!

- Special thanks to Maidenhead Vet Steve Cooke, who made it possible for Bracknell Rabbit Rescue Centre to succeed. With his help and generosity they managed to re-home over 700 bunnies in their four years there.

14348001R00039

Printed in Great Britain
by Amazon.co.uk, Ltd.,
Marston Gate.